0 2015

FREE PUBLIC LIBRARY
133 ELM STREET
NEW HAVEN, CT 06510

SEASON TO SEASON

NATURE'S CYCLES

Jason Cooper

Rourke
Publishing LLC
Vero Beach, Florida 32964

© 2007 Rourke Publishing LLC

All rights reserved. No part of this book may be reproduced or utilized in any form or by any means, electronic or mechanical including photocopying, recording, or by any information storage and retrieval system without permission in writing from the publisher.

www.rourkepublishing.com

PHOTO CREDITS: All Photographs © Lynn M. Stone, except p.6 © NASA and p11 © Nick Bird

Editor: Robert Stengard-Olliges

Cover and interior design by Nicola Stratford

Library of Congress Cataloging-in-Publication Data

Cooper, Jason.
  Season to season / Jason Cooper.
    p. cm. -- (Nature's cycle)
  ISBN 1-60044-181-5 (hardcover)
  ISBN 1-59515-539-2 (softcover)
  1. Seasons--Juvenile literature. 2. Earth--Rotation--Juvenile literature. I. Title. II. Series: Cooper, Jason. Nature's cycle.

QB637.4.S76 2007
508.2--dc22   2006014430

Printed in the USA

CG/CG

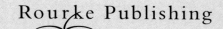

Rourke Publishing

www.rourkepublishing.com – sales@rourkepublishing.com
Post Office Box 3328, Vero Beach, FL 32964

Table of Contents

Four Seasons

Each year has four periods called seasons. They are spring, summer, autumn, and winter.

Each season brings change. The weather changes.
The amount of daylight changes.

The Earth in Motion

Seasons change because of the Earth's motion. The Earth travels through space around the sun.

One journey around the sun takes about 365 days. One year is 365 days.

The Earth's position toward the sun changes each day during its trip. In summer, the northern **hemisphere** faces the sun more directly.

Then the northern half of Earth receives more sunlight.
More sunlight means warmer air.

Meanwhile, the southern hemisphere has its fall and winter. During our fall and winter, the southern half of Earth has spring and summer.

In Australia, for example, the seasons are the
opposite of ours. January in Australia is summer time!

Seasonal Changes

Seasonal changes are different from one place to another.

A big seasonal change in most of North America is air temperature.

In places further south the amount of rainfall is a big seasonal change. Air temperatures do not change much close to the equator.

Seasonal changes bring changes in the lives of plants and animals. More sunlight and warmer spring air start new life in spring.

Plants grow and make flowers. Birds and insects
hatch. Animals grow more active.

Seeds ripen in summer. Young animals grow up.

In autumn the Earth receives less sunlight on the northern half. The air cools. Plants die. Most animals **migrate** south or hide away.

Fall brings colder air and even less sunlight. But the Earth is moving. Winter is just weeks away.

21

Glossary

hatch (HATCH) — when an animal breaks out of
  its egg
hemisphere (HEM uhss fihr) — one half of the earth
migrate (MYE grate) — to move from one region
  to another
seasonal (SEE zuhn uhl) — related to the four seasons
  of the year

INDEX

FURTHER READING

Branley, Franklyn M. *Sunshine Makes the Seasons*. Harper Collins Children's
     Books, 2005.
Pipe, Jim. *Seasons*. Stargazer Books, 2005.

WEBSITES TO VISIT

http://www.woodlands-junior.kent.sch.uk/time/index.html

ABOUT THE AUTHOR:

Jason Cooper has written many children's books for Rourke Publishing about a
variety of topics. Cooper travels widely to gather information for his books.

NEW HAVEN FREE PUBLIC LIBRARY

11   07